HOW TO DRAW
Musical Instruments

Barbara Soloff Levy

DOVER PUBLICATIONS, INC.
Mineola, New York

Note

Have you ever played a musical instrument? Maybe you have taken piano or guitar lessons at home or have played in the school band. Even if you have not, you know that listening to the sounds produced by musical instruments is one of the true joys of life.

Using the thirty step-by-step instruction pages in this book, you will learn to draw musical instruments such as a piano, an electric guitar, a clarinet, and even a pair of maracas! Each instruction page has several steps, usually three or four. First, draw the basic shapes shown in the first step. For the rest of the steps, add details to your pictures as shown. The last step shows you what the finished drawing looks like. It's a good idea to trace the steps first, just to get a feel for drawing. Use a pencil with an eraser in case you want to make any changes along the way. You will see dotted lines in some of the pictures—erase these lines as a final step. You'll find a helpful Practice Page with plenty of space opposite each set of steps, too. When you are pleased with your drawing, you may wish to go over the lines with a felt-tip pen or colored pencil. Finally, feel free to color your drawings any way you wish.

After you have finished drawing the pictures in this book, why not use your new skills to create more drawings of your very own? Have fun!

Copyright

Copyright © 2009 by Barbara Soloff Levy
All rights reserved.

Bibliographical Note

How to Draw Musical Instruments is a new work, first published by Dover Publications, Inc., in 2009.

International Standard Book Number

ISBN-13: 978-0-486-46220-2
ISBN-10: 0-486-46220-X

Manufactured in the United States of America
Dover Publications, Inc., 31 East 2nd Street, Mineola, N.Y. 11501

HOW TO DRAW
Musical Instruments

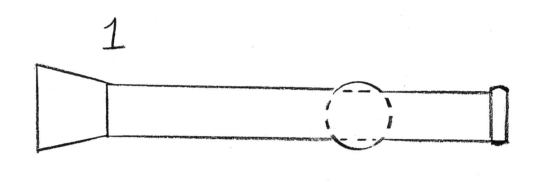

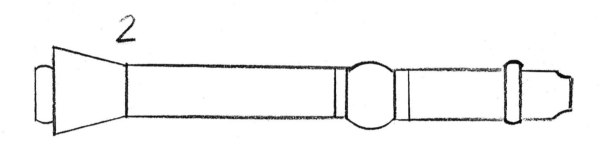

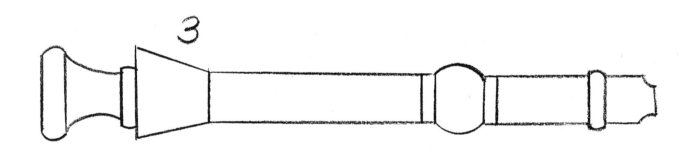

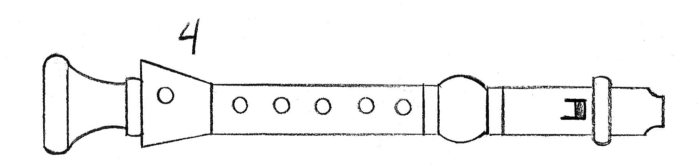

Practice Page

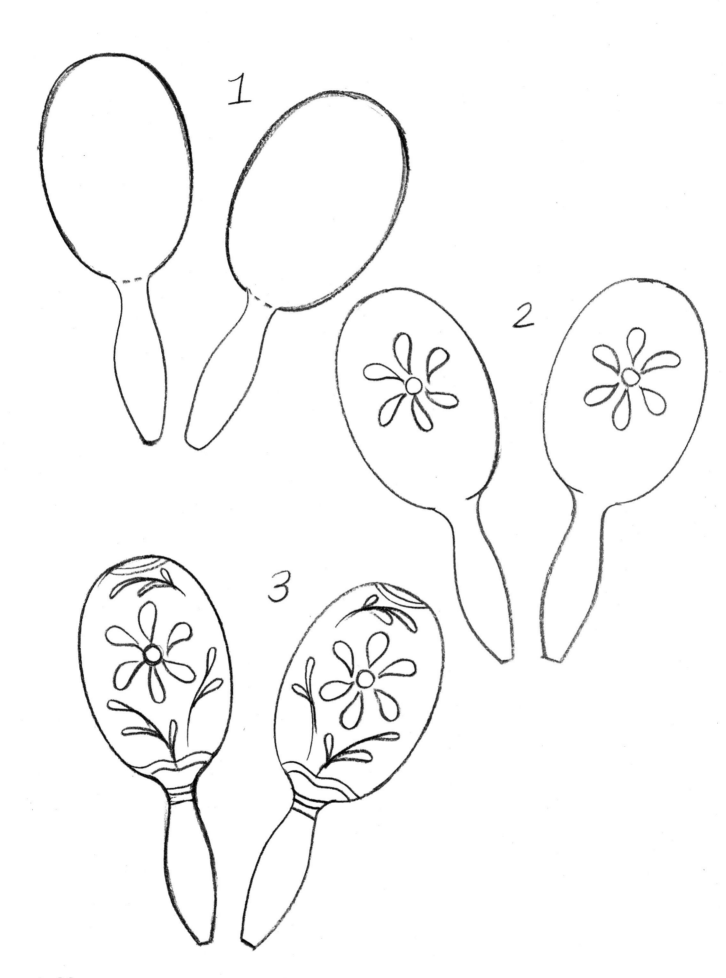

1

2

3

4   Maracas

Practice Page

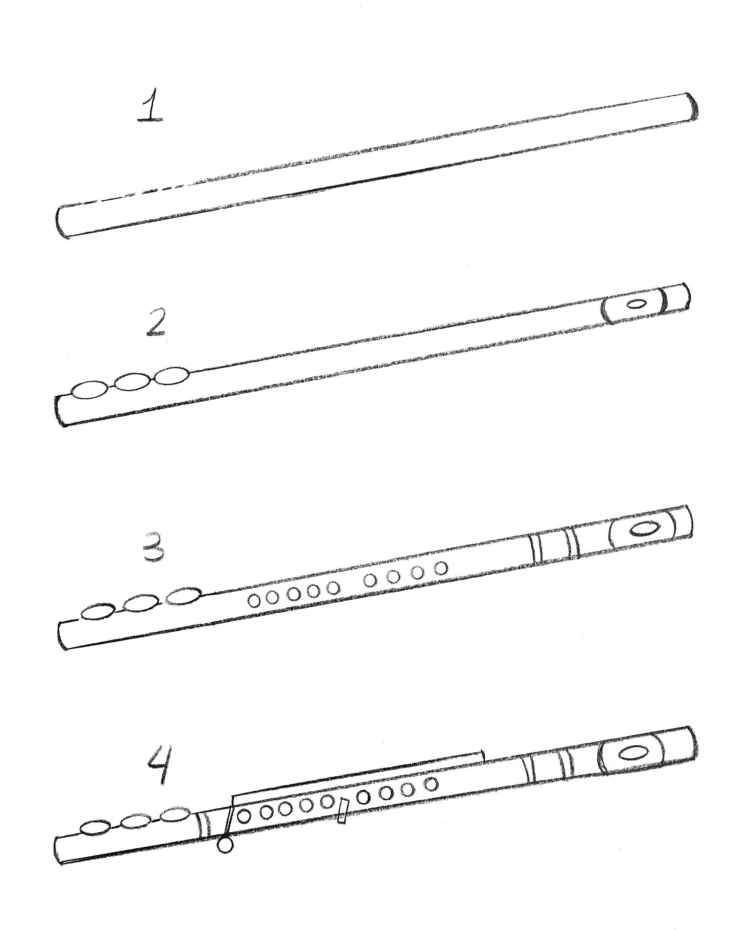

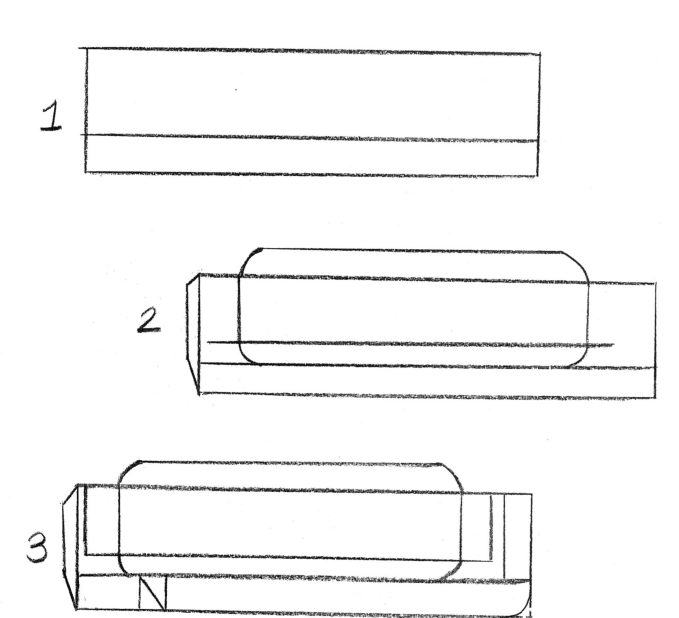

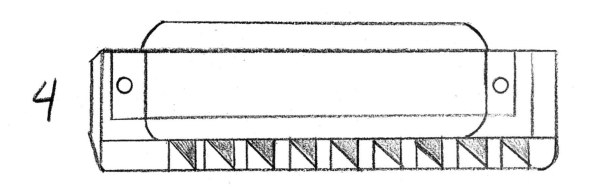

Practice Page

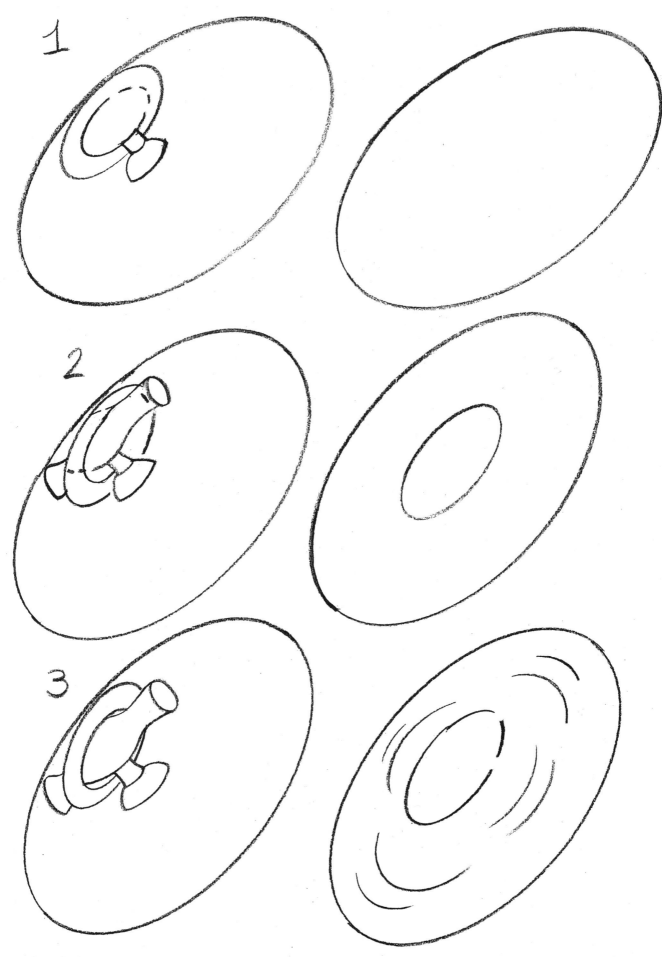

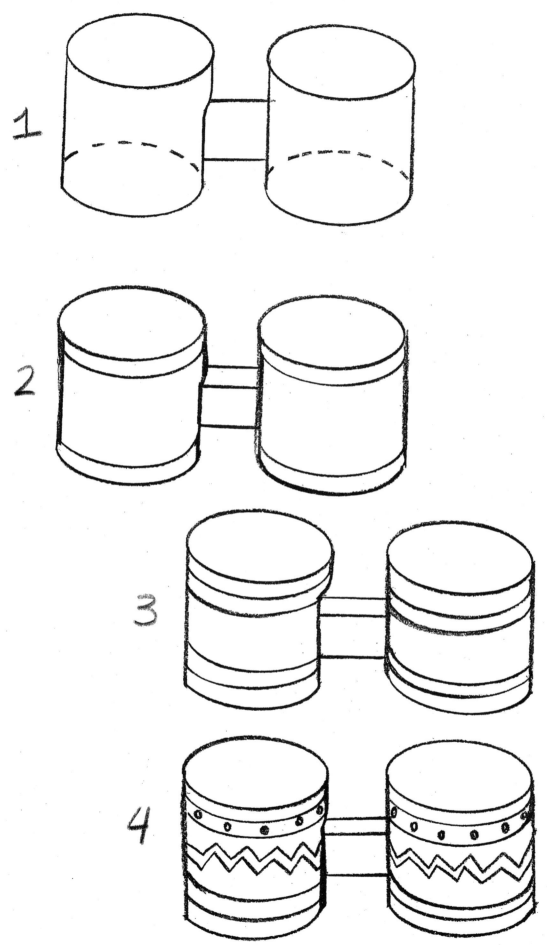

Practice Page

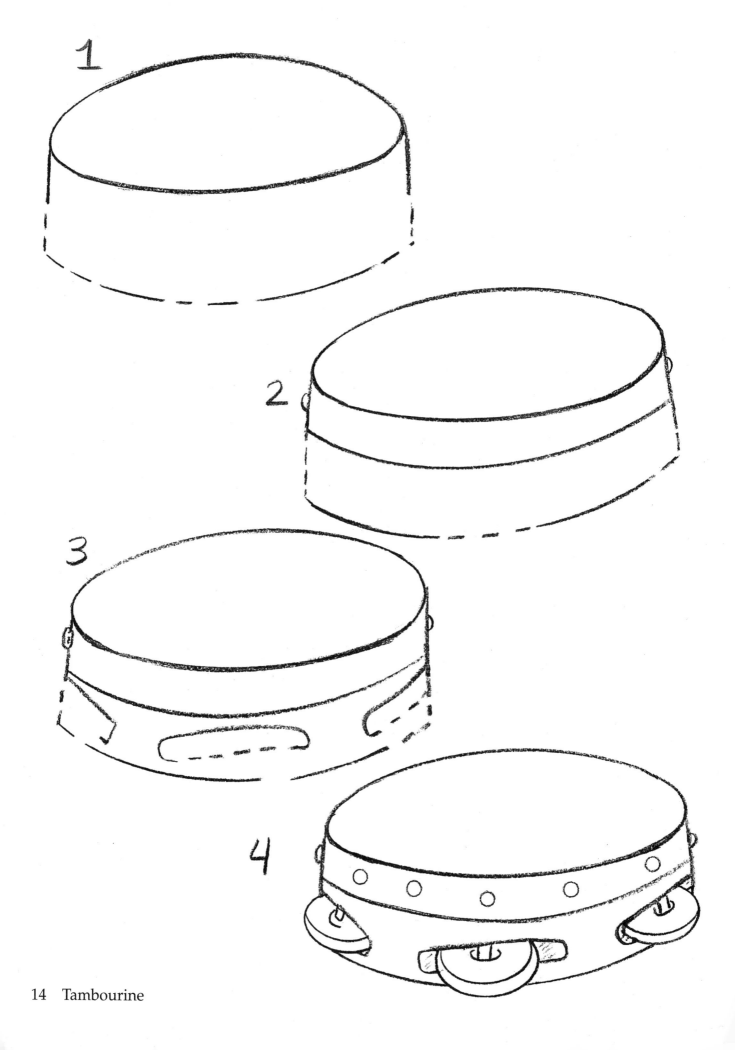

1

2

3

4

14   Tambourine

Practice Page

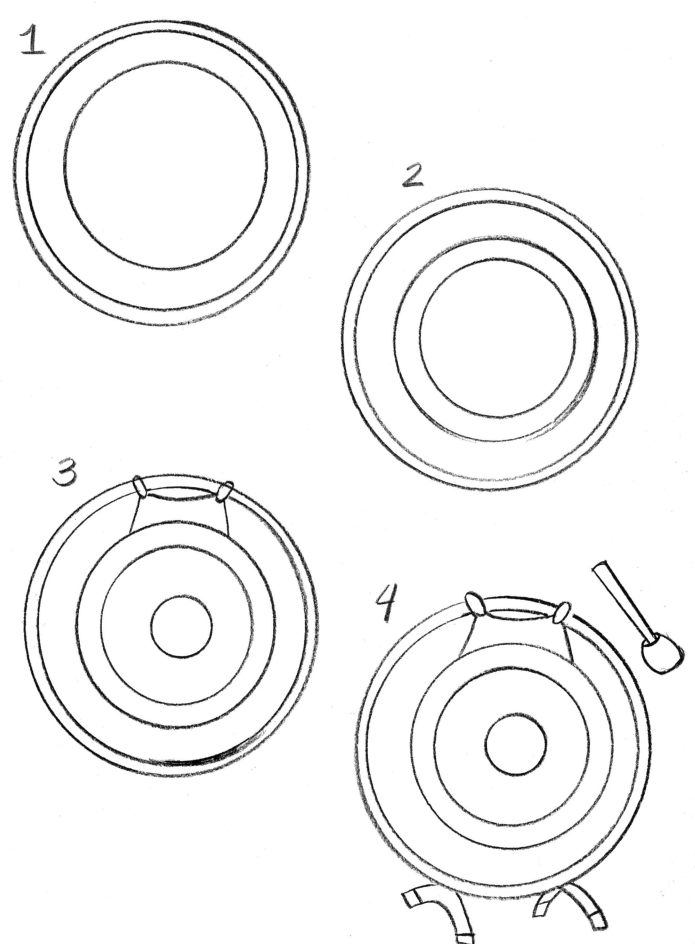

1

2

3

4

Practice Page

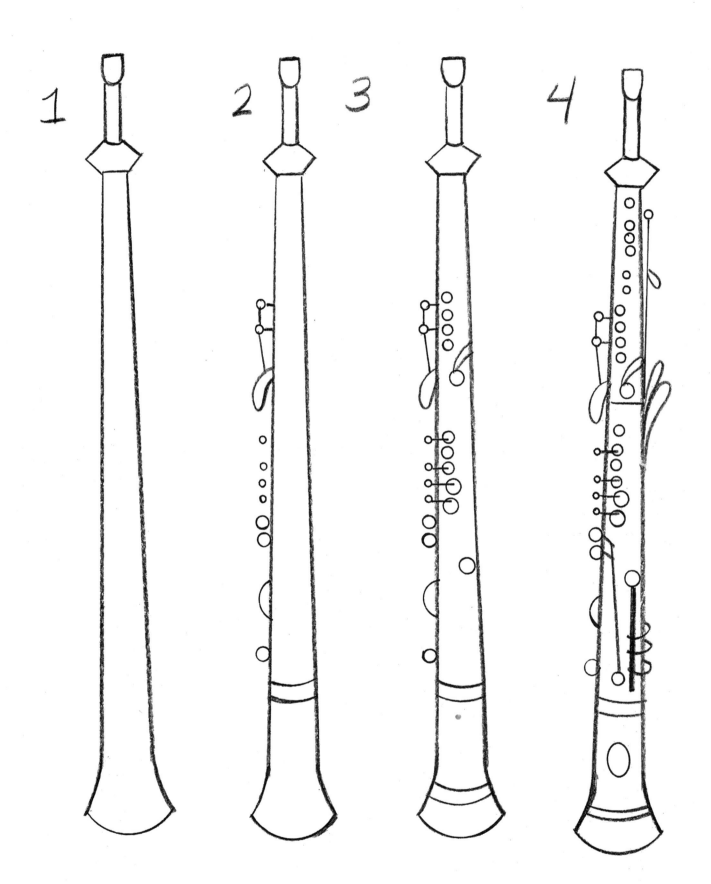

18 Oboe

Practice Page

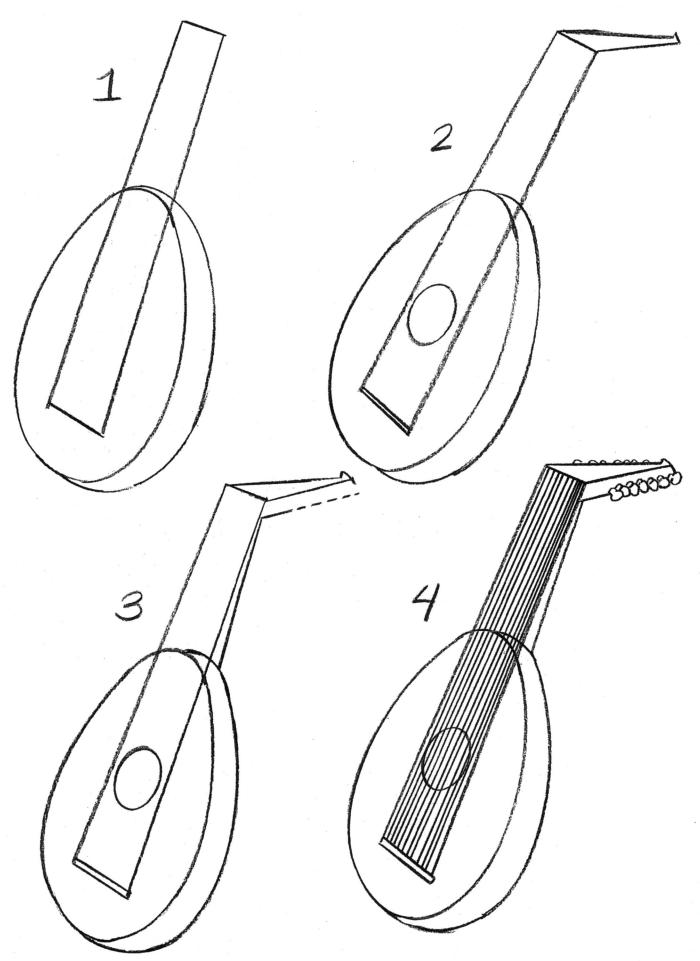

Practice Page

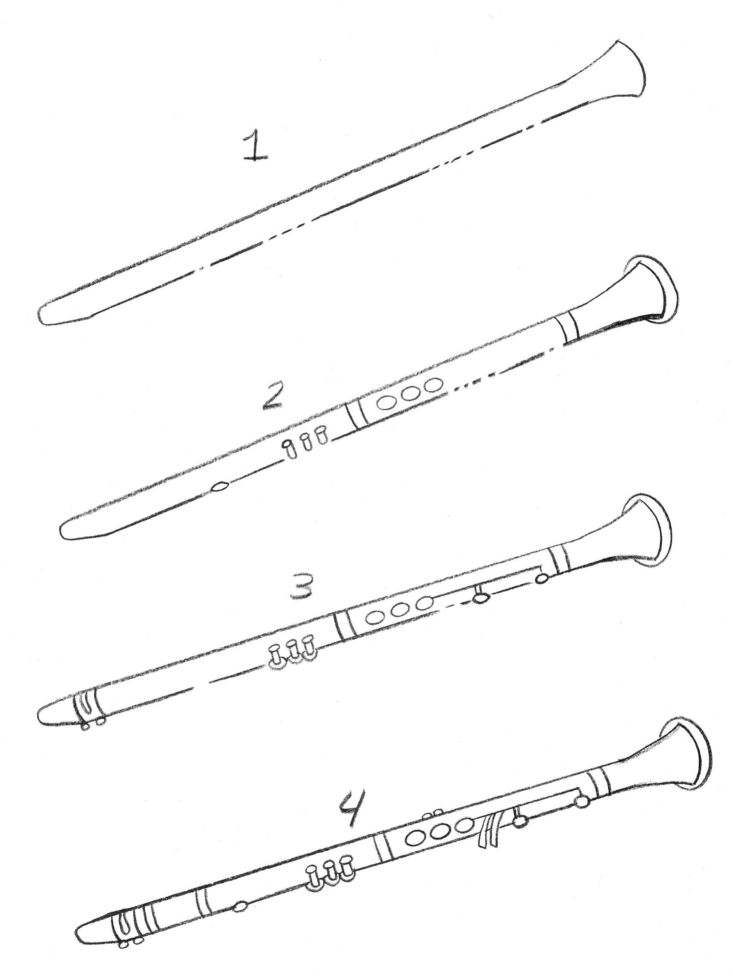

1

2

3

4

Practice Page

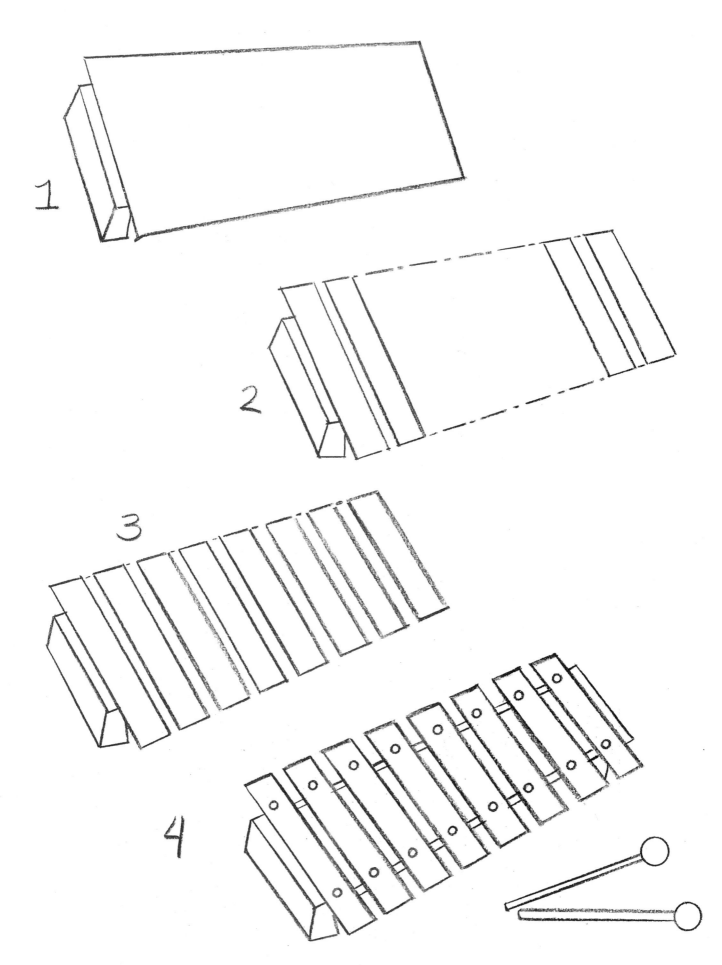

1

2

3

4

Practice Page

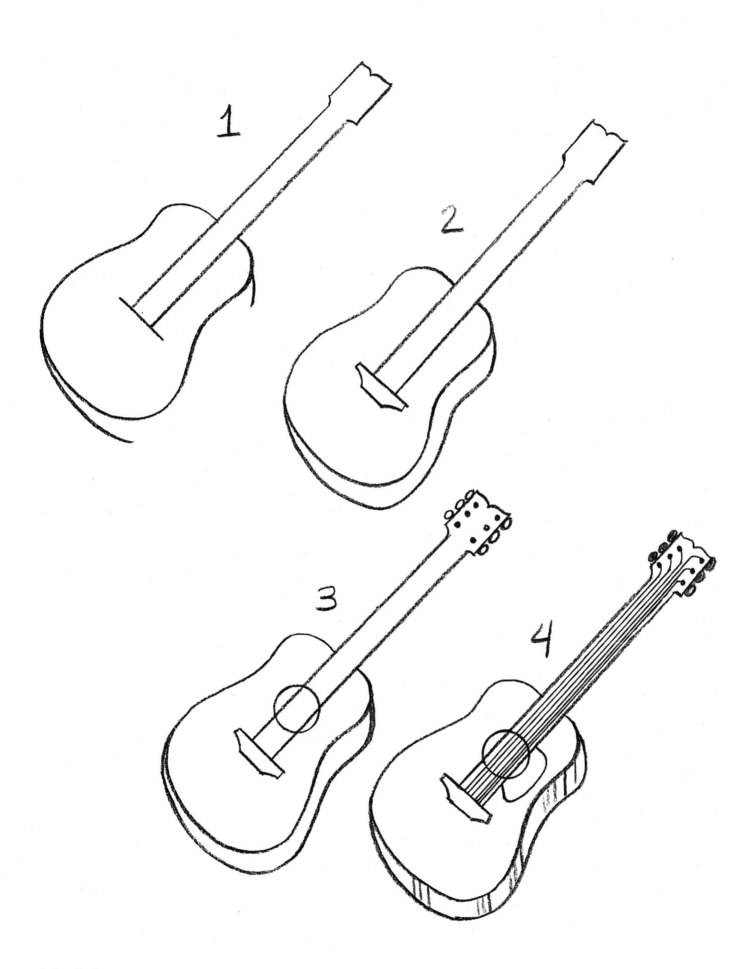

1

2

3

4

Practice Page

1

2

3

4

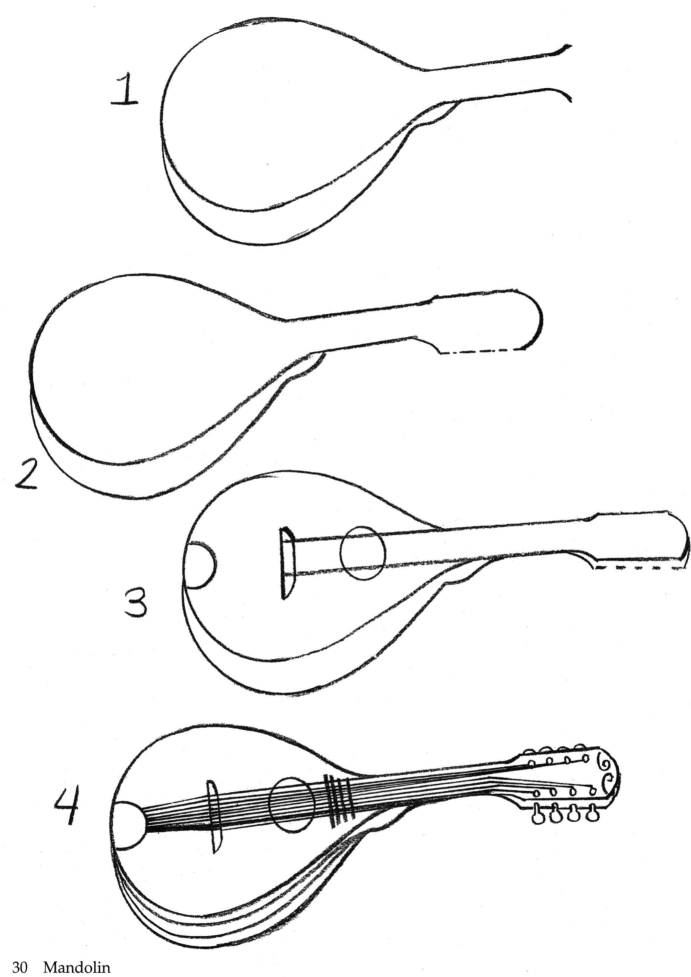

1

2

3

4

Practice Page

Practice Page

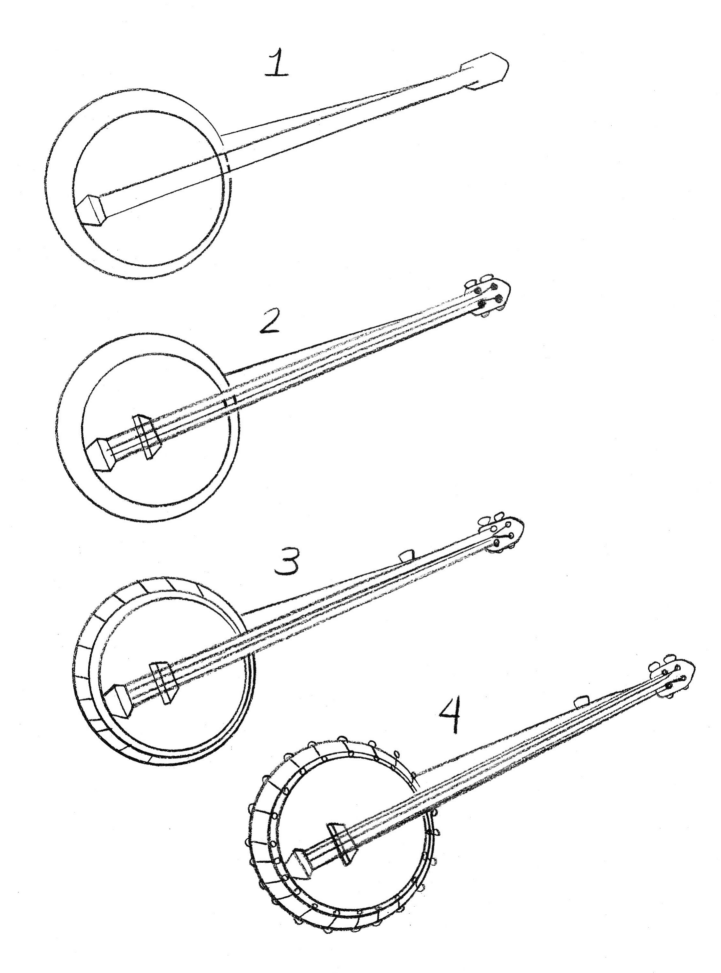

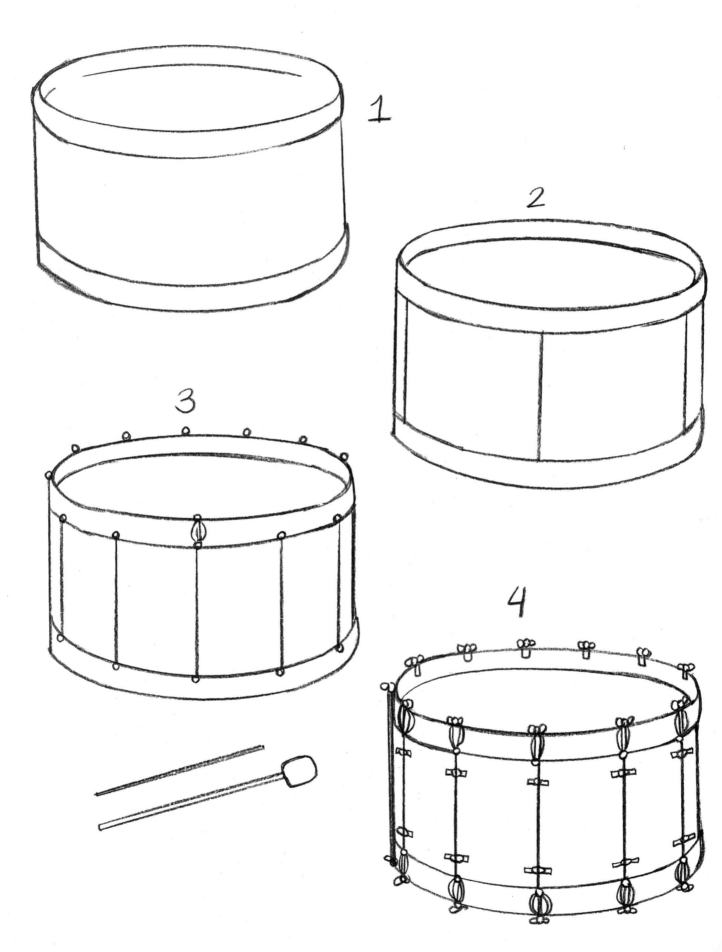

1

2

3

4

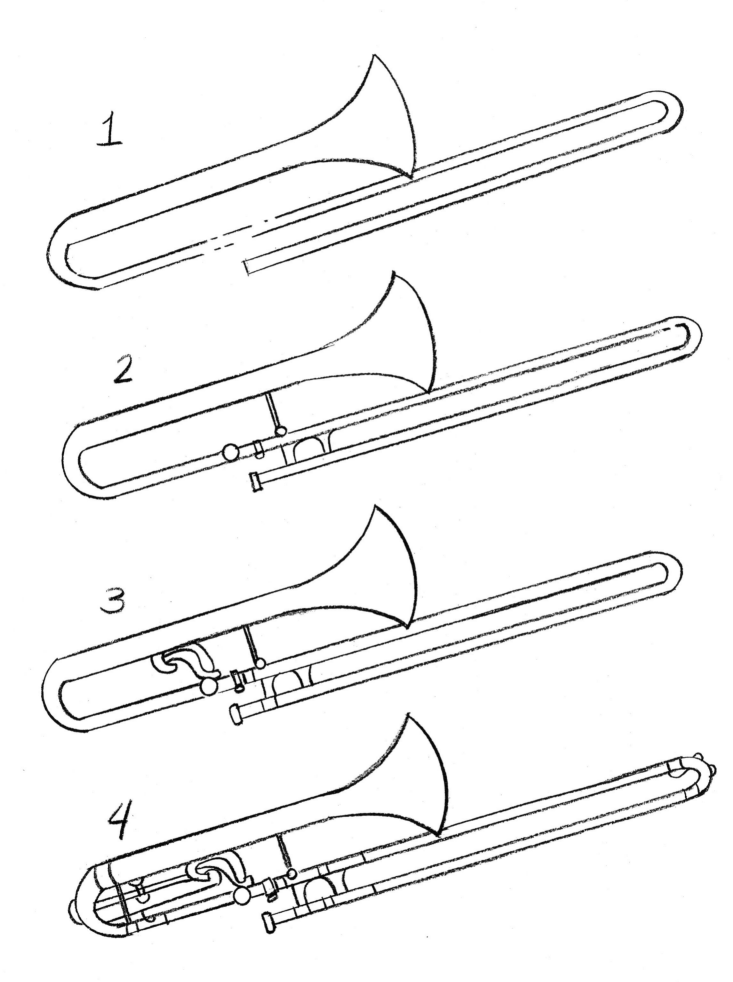

Practice Page

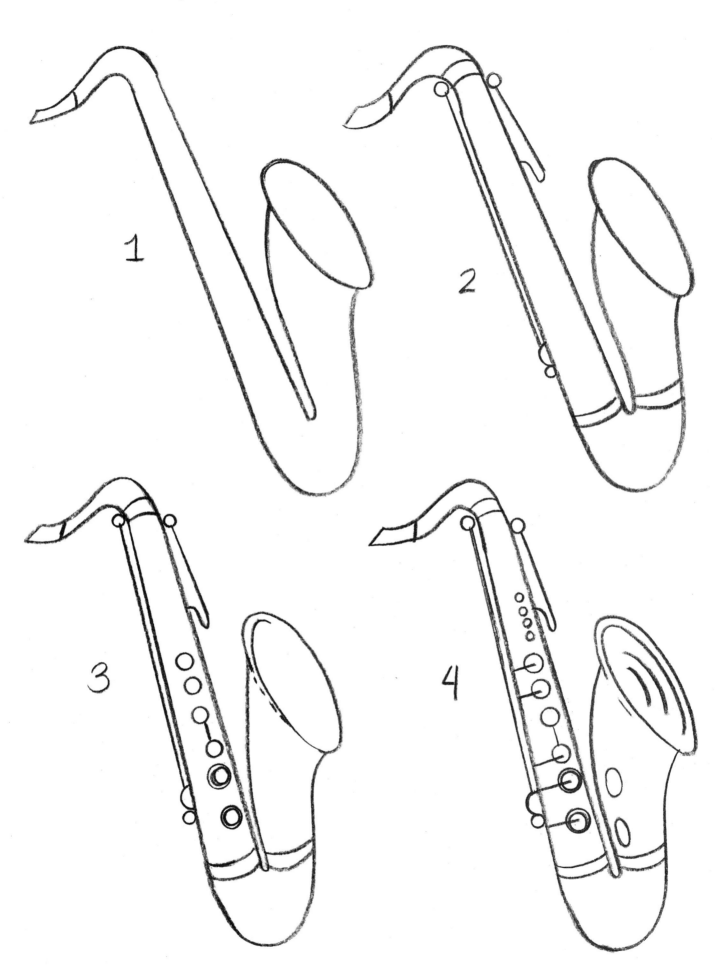

1

2

3

4

Practice Page

40   Cello (or Double Bass)

Practice Page

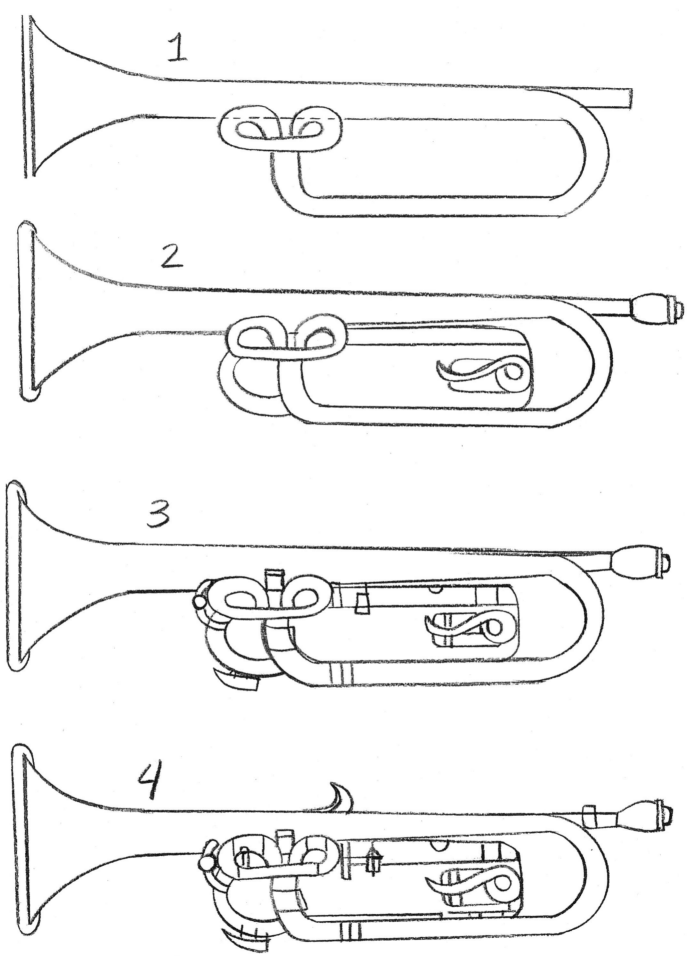

Practice Page

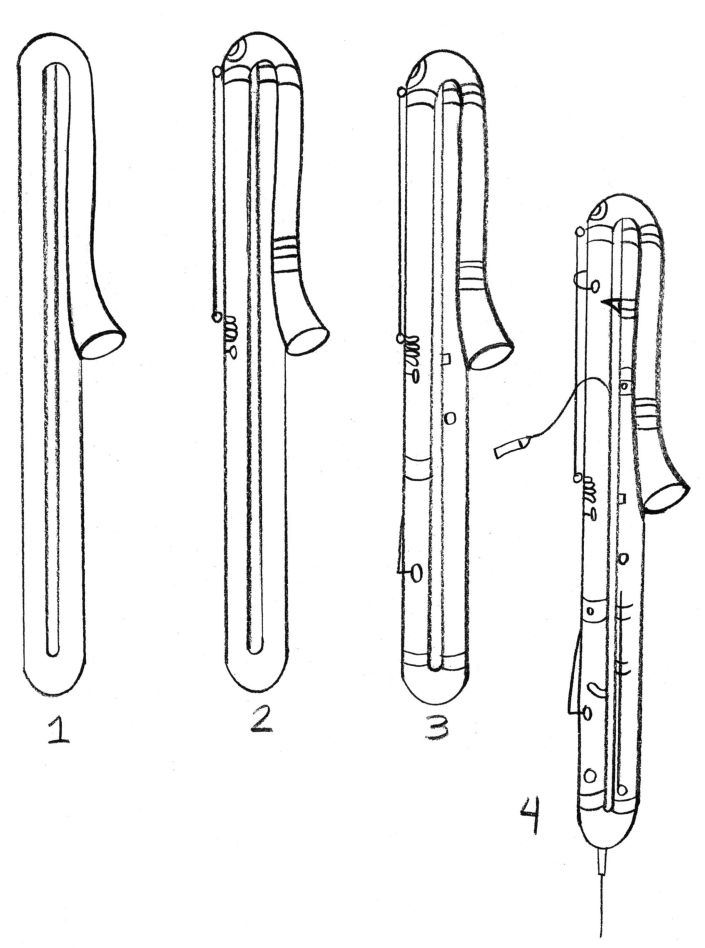

1

2

3

4

Practice Page

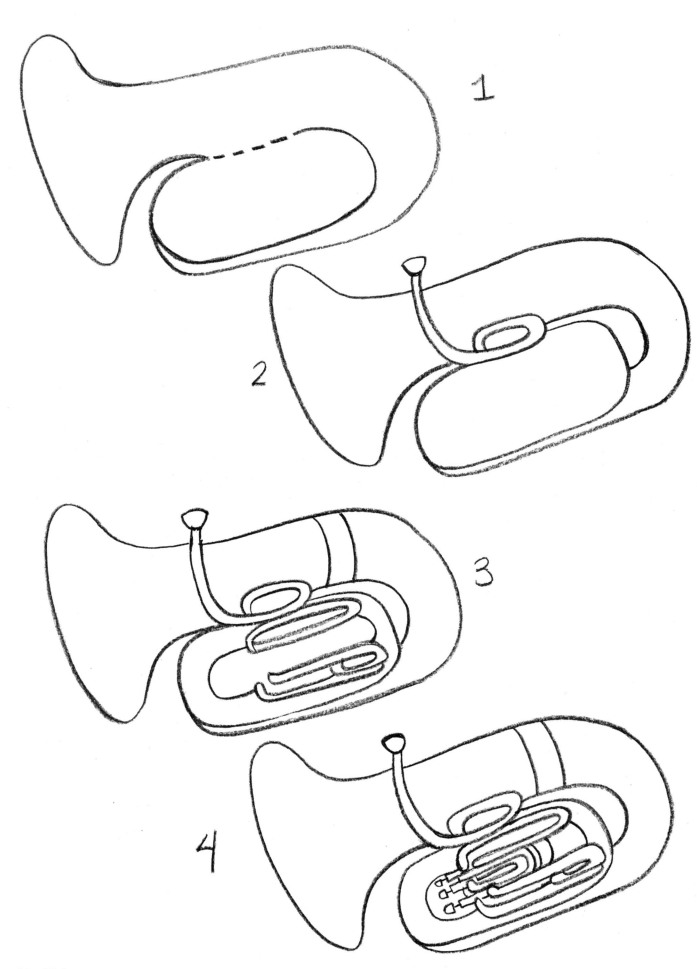

1

2

3

4

Practice Page

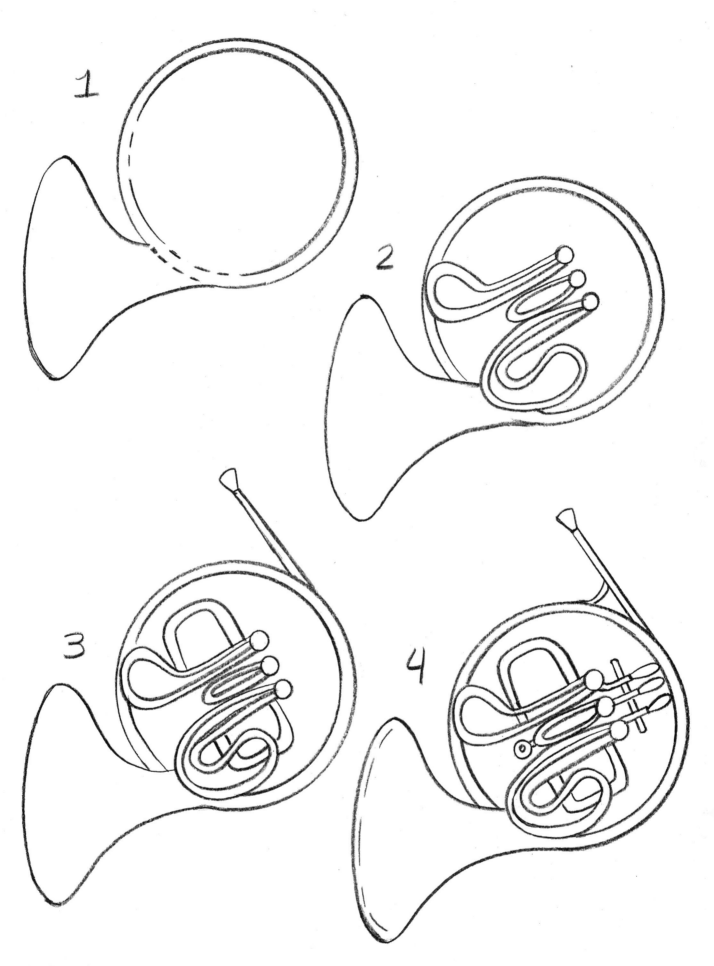

1

2

3

4

Practice Page

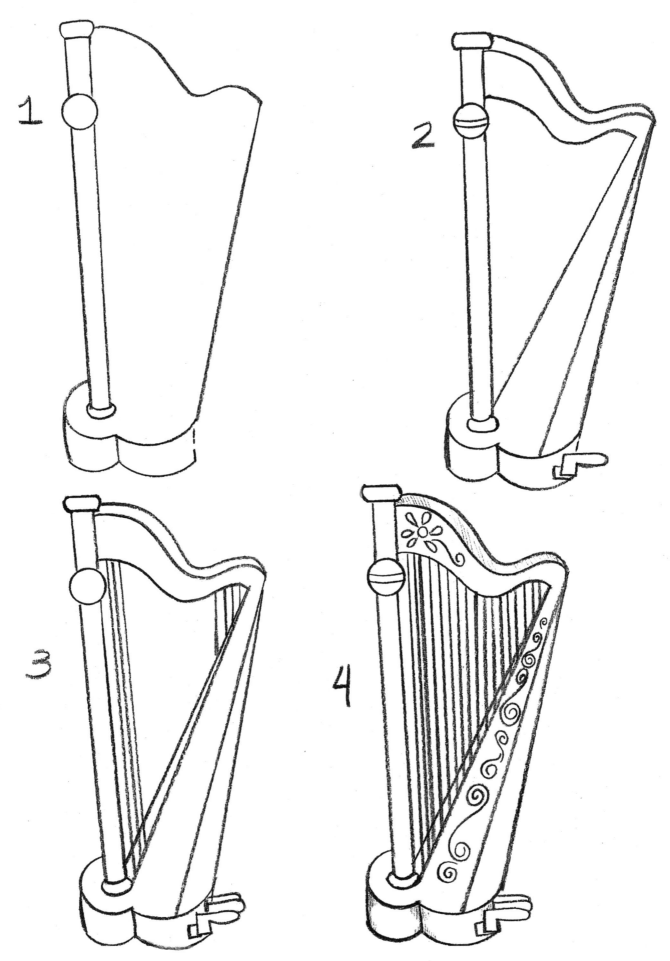

52   Harp

Practice Page

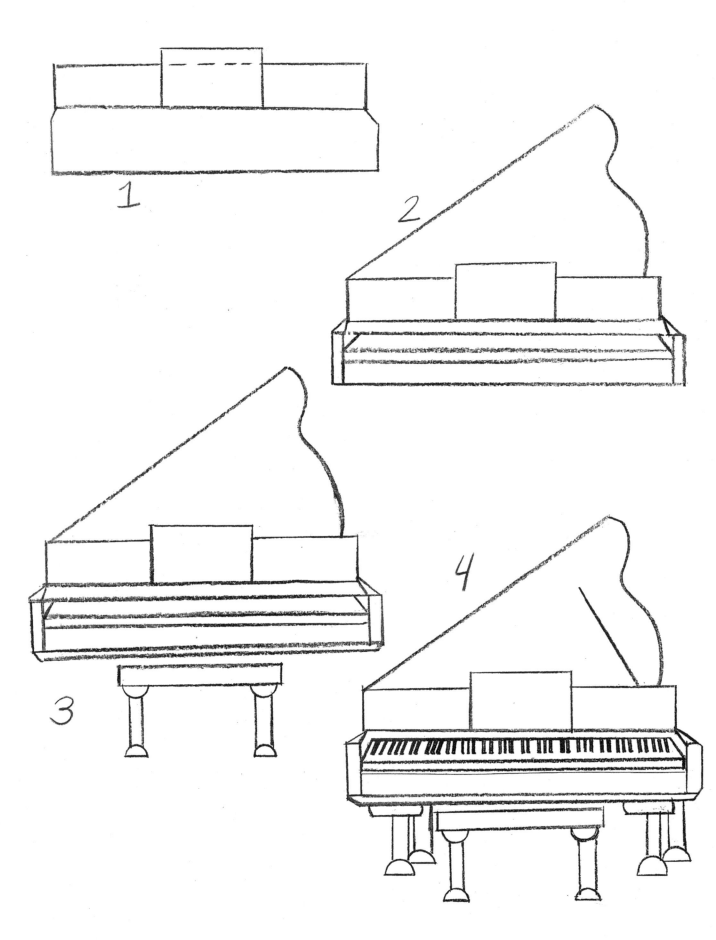

1

2

3

4

Practice Page

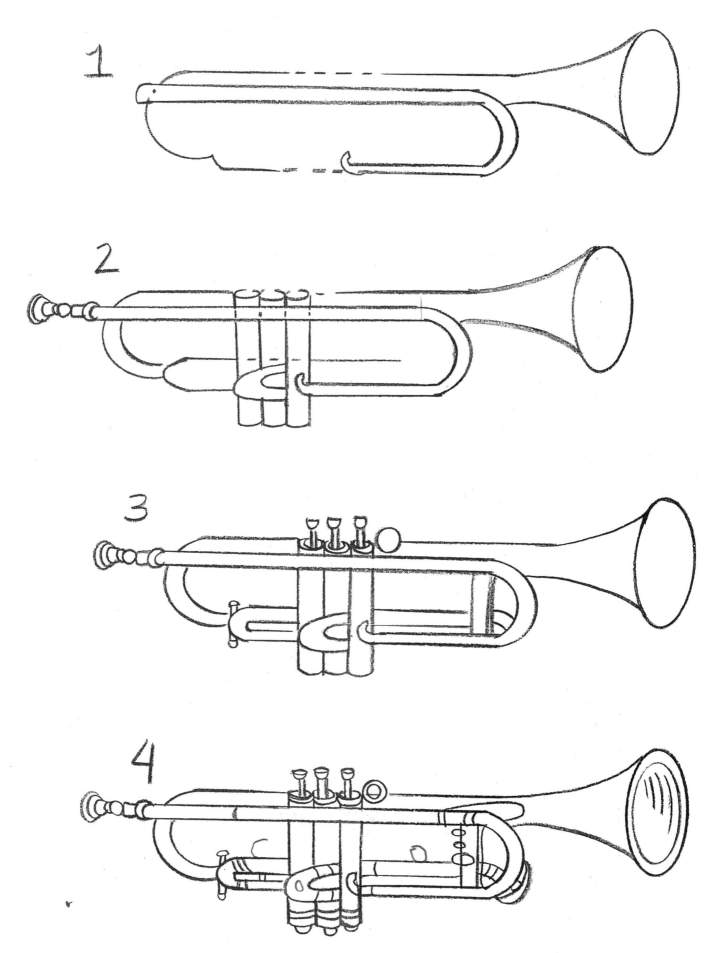

Practice Page

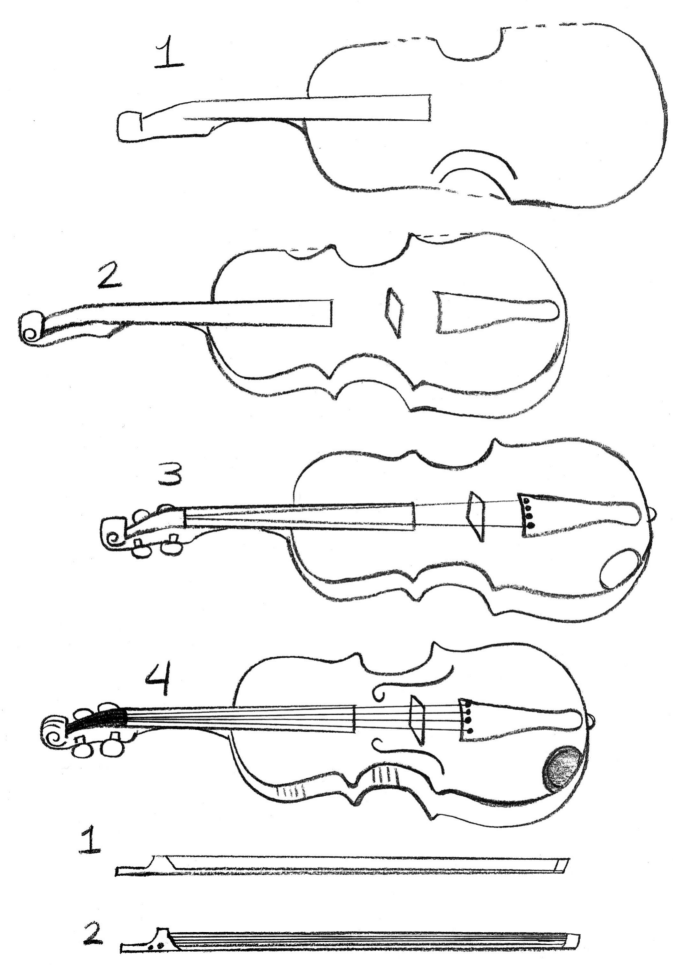

58 Violin

Practice Page

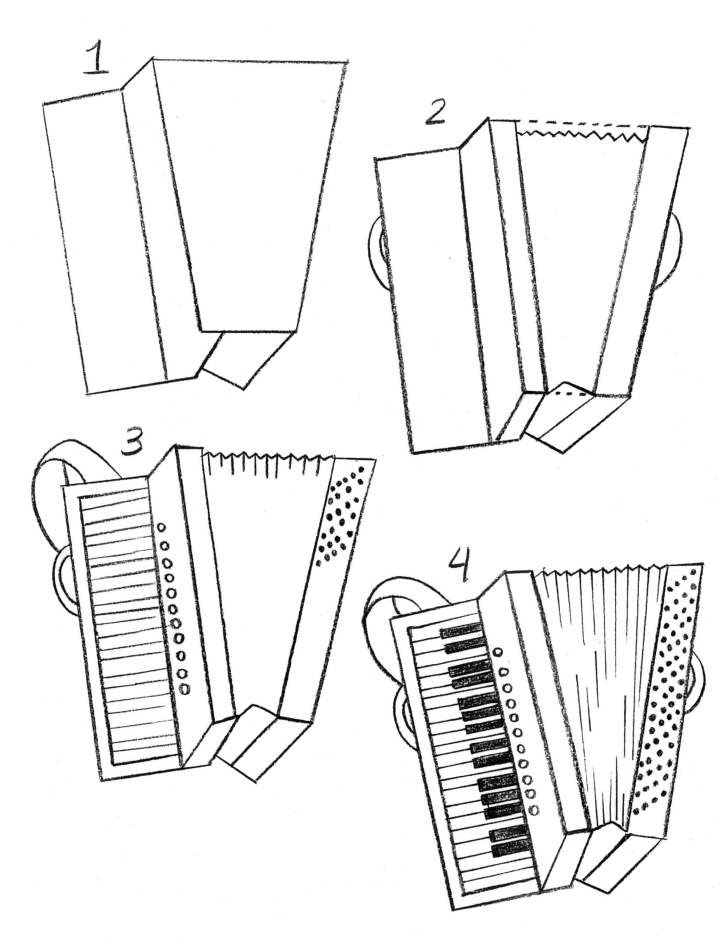

Practice Page